Escape of the Giant Chicken

Jan Burchett and Sara Vogler ✳ Jonatronix

OXFORD
UNIVERSITY PRESS

In this story ...

Max

Cat

Ant

Tiger

Shelly
the chicken

Max, Cat, Ant and Tiger were visiting the local city farm. They were the first visitors to get there.

"I'm glad we are here early," said Max.

"We'll have lots of time to see everything," said Cat eagerly.

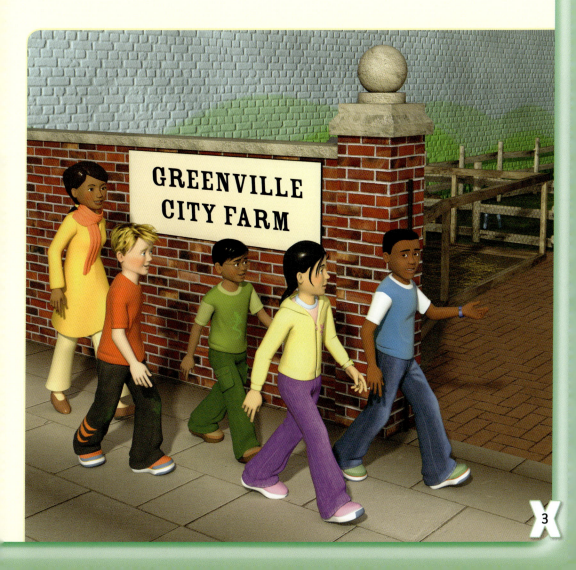

GREENVILLE CITY FARM

They stopped at the chicken pen. Ant bought some corn to feed them with.

The biggest chicken was called Shelly. As soon as Ant threw down some corn, Shelly darted over and gobbled it up.

"She's so greedy," laughed Ant.

"Chickens are boring," said Tiger. "They never do anything exciting."

Tiger looked over the next fence. One of the farm helpers was milking a cow. She asked Tiger if he would like to try.

"Yeah!" said Tiger.

Max, Cat and Ant came over to watch.

Tiger sat on a stool next to the cow. The woman showed him what to do.

"Easy!" he said.

But it was not as easy as it looked. Instead of hitting the bucket, the jet of milk shot off to one side. *SPLAT!* It hit Ant on the arm.

"There's something wrong with this cow!" muttered Tiger.

Hey!

"There's something wrong with the milker!" grumbled Ant. "I'm soaked!"

"Oh, dear," said the woman. "You'll need to wash it off."

The woman helped Tiger back over the fence. She showed the children to the sink and gave them some soap to clean up with. Then she went off to find a towel.

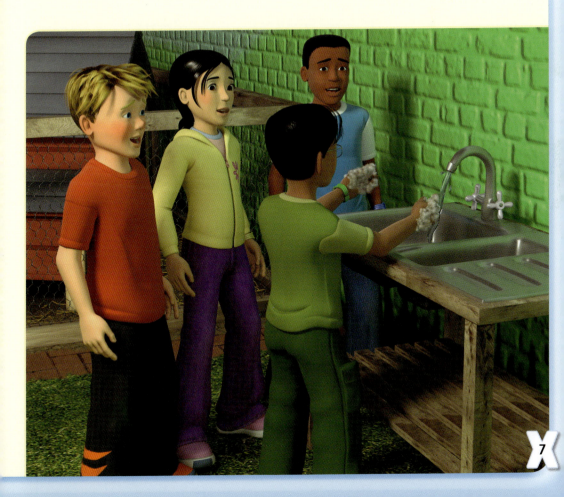

Ant was in a sulk. He went back to look at the chickens. It was just then that his watch began to crackle. Some of the milk had got into his watch!

Suddenly a green beam shot out from Ant's watch towards the chicken pen. It hit Shelly in the chest.

"Oh, no!" cried Cat.

Shelly began
to grow …
and grow …
and grow!

The giant chicken squawked. Then she flapped out of the pen and over the wall of the farm. The farm backed on to the big park.

"We have to get her back and shrink her," yelled Max, "before anyone sees."

"We have to catch her first!" said Ant.

Shelly was halfway across the park by the time the children got there. She had already destroyed a flowerbed and a football net.

"She's heading for the café," said Ant.

"Someone will see her!" groaned Max.

The children raced after the chicken. Shelly ran round the back of the café and began pecking at some old food in a bin.

"We'll creep up on her," Max told them. "Follow me."

They tiptoed closer. But the chicken's sharp eyes saw them coming. She flapped up on to the café roof.

"That worked well," scoffed Tiger.

"Any better ideas?" asked Max, crossly.

Shelly began to scratch at the café roof. "She's trying to dig a hole!" gasped Cat. "No, she's not," said Ant, as Shelly sat down. "She's laying an egg!"

Shelly clucked proudly. She stood up and a giant egg rolled out from underneath her. It rolled down the roof and … *SPLAT!* It hit the ground.

"We've been scrambled!" groaned Tiger.

People in the café were now beginning to look round to see where the clucking was coming from. The children cleaned themselves off.

"We can't leave Shelly up there," said Max, wiping yolk off his face.

"I wish I had some corn left," said Ant. "We could tempt her down."

Shelly was perched on the edge of the roof, looking for something else to eat.

"We may not have any corn," said Max, "but I know something that might work."

He ran off into the café and was soon back with a large, paper bag.

"Bread rolls," Max said, handing them out.

"Egg-cellent idea!" joked Tiger.

Max waved a roll at the chicken. Shelly caught sight of the bread.

"Get ready to grab her," Max said.

He threw his roll on the ground. The others did the same.

With a greedy cluck, Shelly jumped to the ground. Cat grabbed her round the leg.

"Got you!" she yelled.

"*SQUAWK!*" screeched Shelly.

The giant chicken ran off along the path with Cat hanging on.

Cat had a bumpy ride. She needed to shrink so Shelly would shrink too.

Cat managed to turn the dial on her watch but she still needed to press the button in the middle.

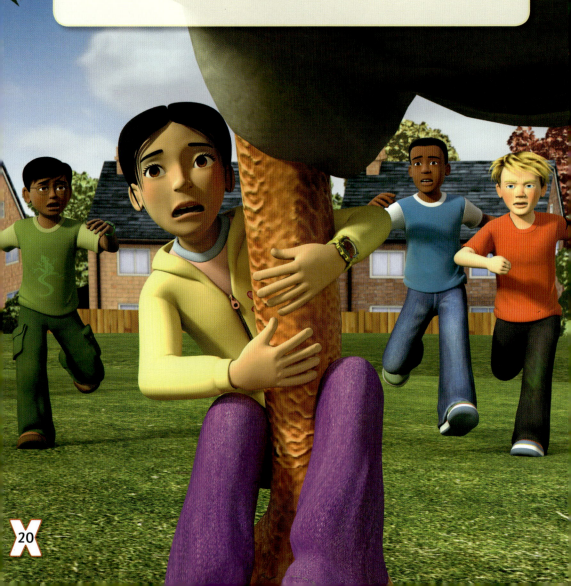

Shelly was getting faster and Cat had to hold on with both hands. Then Cat had a brainwave. She pressed her nose down hard on her watch and …

Max and Ant blocked the chicken's path and Tiger picked her up. He held her gently, making sure her wings could not flap around.

Cat grew back to normal size. They hurried back to the farm. Tiger put Shelly back in her pen. The chicken gave him an angry glare and strutted off.

"That was egg-citing," Tiger said, with a grin. He looked over at the cow again. "I might have another go at milking."

"Hide, everyone!" yelled Max.

"What's the matter?" laughed Tiger. "Are you chicken?"

Yolk page ...

Why did the chicken cross the road?

To get to the other side.

Why did the chicken cross the playground?

To get to the other slide.

What do you get when you cross a chicken with a bell?

An alarm cluck.

Which side of a chicken has the most feathers?

The outside!